Broken

Pews

~Broken To Minister

Suicidal Thoughts

Anxiety   Depression

Family & Friends   Church   Relationships

Ka'teteia Simmons

ISBN: 978-1-943409-62-4
All Rights Reserved

Pure Thoughts Publishing, LLC

Contents

Acknowledgments 5

Dedication 7

BROKEN IN TWO 8

WHERE THE CRACK STARTED 13

LIFE APPLICATION..20

WHY DOES IT HURT SO BAD? 22

LIFE APPLICATION..28

I THOUGHT I WAS OVER IT 30

LIFE APPLICATION..34

LET IT GO..37

LIFE APPLICATION..45

THE FLIP SIDE OF PAIN 48

LIFE APPLICATION..52

BROKEN PEW 55

LIFE APPLICATION..61

PARABLE OF PRUNING.......................................64

LIFE APPLICATION..68

THE BLESSING OF BROKENNESS 70

BROKEN TO MINISTER..74

FREE TO BE BROKEN 76

CONCLUSION 78

BROKEN PEWS:

BROKEN TO MINISTER

By:

KA'TETCIA KING-SIMMONS

Acknowledgments

A special thank you to God for bringing this vision to pass, for choosing me to be a catalyst of healing for a hurting generation, and for being the awesome God he is.

A special thank you to my coach, Marita Kinney, and the Pure Thoughts Publishing family for believing in me and helping to propel me into my purpose.

A special thank you to my editors,Chrissy Cutting and "The Purple Pen Editor," D'Jaris Mack, for not only utilizing her talents but making certain I remained grounded and balanced during this entire project.

A special thank you to my Mom, Charlesena King; my sister, Janice King; and my brother, Michael King, for not only their love and support but giving me that extra push.

A very special thank you to the late Pastor Elder Rodney B. James, my spiritual "Papi" for always reminding me to pick up the pieces and "Never QUIT." Also, to my diamond, Lady Carla A. James for being that clear-cut valuable jewel she is to me, always having the right words to say and the love she shares at all times.

A very special thank you to my friends (Lisa Felder, LuKeesha Pearson, Pastor DeSheka James, and Pastor Kimberly King) who had to hear and witness me through some of the most challenging and broken stages in my life. I am grateful and so appreciative that none of you gave up on me, threw me away or even judged me. Rather, you always gave me hope and encouragement that I could make it. You each are truly a part of my village—for you each helped me to grow and become so much better. Love you all to life.

Dedication

This book is dedicated to my husband, Rodney O. Simmons—my knight in shining armor, my king, my lover, my friend. A man who saw past my hurt and pain enough to love me as deeply as Christ loved the church. A man who helped me discover the "flip side of being broken" through loving me to life. I appreciate and am ever so grateful to you for helping to heal my heart with your undying and unconditional love.

BROKEN IN TWO

Historically, pews were non-existent. There is really no evidence to support pews even being in the early church. The early church had standing room only. Churchgoers could kneel or stand as they worshiped. Yes, the entire gathering consisted of them standing or kneeling. So, we must be very careful and most appreciative now when we complain about our current pews, right?

When pews first became popular, they were very simple yet sturdy. They were made of mostly two main planks of wood that were held together by a handful of nails (much like the cross just positioned differently in its fastenings). Yet, it created a place for churchgoers to sit and hear the Word of God. Unlike today, pews were bought and paid for by wealthy families of the congregation who actually held deeds to them as if they were real estate. Rich congregants demanded more space for luxurious style pews. While poorer congregants kept being crammed into smaller and smaller spaces. This caused churches to become more and more expensive to build and fund. Eventually, most churches did away with those elaborate stadium-style box pews and replaced them with the free and open wooden bench style that we see today.

Though the physical pew can be uncomfortable, it was really meant to be comforting. The pew is now considered a very integral piece of furnishing of a church. Traditionally, some say it is forbidden to even change them. Some people see the pews as having that spiritual connection with those who have worshipped there before. Along with the strength of pews, flexibility and comfort add to their purpose. Families can be seated together. Couples can be seated together. Larger persons can have more room. More space can be provided for a larger crowd as well. Sometimes, so much is done with pews that it causes a lot of wear and tear and leads to them being damaged or broken.

So, we will take a journey through these next few pages of the wear and tear of pews (you & I). Yes, as the old saying goes . . . there is only so much a person can take before one's life becomes broken. I would still like to remind you as you read these pages that no matter what, you are still very integral in the kingdom. You are an important part of the lives of others as well. You may have been broken before and possibly are still experiencing some brokenness—just know that there is still a purpose for you in the kingdom. No matter where you started or how, someone else's deliverance lies inside of you.

There may have been times when you were hurt by not only friends but those closest to you. You may even think back to times when you have given so much of yourself in relationships and friendships only to find that you were being misused or abused. You then think to yourself and wonder how you could let this happen.

Sometimes you may have even felt that you were the only one "going through this." Everyone and everything around you seemed to be going well. Everyone else was being blessed. You were the only one that seemed to always have a valley experience. It came to the point that you just got so tired of being around folks that were always prospering and doing well. Nothing seemed to go wrong for them. You started feeling alone, so lonely. You even said "no one understands" or "no one cares" or even "this has never happened to anyone else."

Well, my friend, the truth of the matter is that we have all had our share of being broken. We have all been through some dark days, hard times, and lonely moments. We all have had experiences of being hurt—in other words, being broken. If you look hard and are completely honest with yourself, some of us are still experiencing some dark days in the valley.

The sad truth is that there is a twofold experience to being broken that we never really hear or teach about. As humans, we naturally only focus on the one side of being broken—the part that hurts. Whether you are the preacher or teacher, the usher or deacon, choir member or musician, or simply a visitor or member on the pew, you have experienced being broken. This is the truth we have all been taught and lived because this is what we have heard over and over again. And yet, this truth we continue to pass down to our children.

There is yet another experience of being broken. I'd like to call it the "flip side of brokenness." This is the side that actually heals the wound. This side is like applying rubbing alcohol to a sore without a scab. It hurts but only to heal. This side of being broken is ointment to wounds that were left from some other form of hurt or pain. We have to learn how to zoom in on healing the hurt rather than the hurt itself. If we learn to focus on the healing, the hurt will appear small and then forgiveness will naturally reign.

This book is about going and growing through a "broken" life. There comes a point in this journey called life when everything fails. No psychiatrist can help. No self-help books work. No spa can spare relief. It is at this point that you reach out to God. This book is about reaching out to God, or so you think, only to find that you are still broken and that healing did not take place when you expected it. This book will expose some valuable truths about being in the church, saved, and helping others only to find yourself still on a broken pew (maybe a broken pew yourself). This book will also share a few testimonials on the two sides of brokenness. Most importantly, as you embark on this journey of "Broken Pews," may the Spirit of God reign over your life, may he lift the Spirit of heaviness, give you beauty from the ashes, and enlarge your territory. Let the healing begin . . .

WHERE THE CRACK STARTED

~Be careful, it's beginning to crack~

"Sticks and stones may break my bones, but words never hurt!" Does that sound familiar? Well, perhaps this one hits home a little more for you: "Blood is thicker than water." These are two very familiar clichés that many of us have heard and adopted as mottos from childhood. Some of us even taught and may even be teaching our children these sayings as if they were some sort of golden rule or Scripture from the Bible.

If the truth be told, in the sense of where or how we learned these "rules" are simple lies and deceptions to cover up some truth or cover up some pain. Let's explore the first: Words do hurt. Folks can say some things to you and about you that will pierce right into your heart. The Word of God reminds us that life and death lie in the power of the tongue. It is one of the smallest yet deadliest instruments of the body. It is more dangerous than using your hands or fist in a physical altercation. When we gossip, lie, or scandalize somebody's name, we just committed murder. We can speak life or speak damnation all with this one little uncontrollable instrument called the tongue.

Take a moment and think back to your greatest revenge on a person. Think about when you really "got them back" for the hurt they caused you. It was when you told them off. Whether you cursed them out or you were just "nice-nasty" or sarcastic, you hurt them. It felt good at the moment because you "got them back." This was the only way to do so without getting into any possible legal trouble. One of the most painful things anyone could do is to say something mean or hurtful to you or about you. So, words do hurt.

The second cliché we hear most often in family battles or rivalries. Maybe an older member of the family will remind you that you are to stick with your blood. You have to protect your kinfolk and do no harm to them because blood is thicker than water. Maybe, a family member is having a disagreement or altercation with one of your friends, you will be reminded to always stick with your blood. In other words, no matter what happens, your blood, your kinfolk should always have your back. They should always look out for you. They should always have your best interest in mind. They should never stab you in the back or cross any lines with you. Your family will be with you through thick and thin. Family should never fuss, fight, argue, or fall out with one another because blood is thicker than water. Whatever happens to one member of the family should happen to all. So, there should be no room for family gossip or negativity within the family.

In all honesty, family will most likely be the first to hurt you or cause you pain. Most American families are more dysfunctional than families in any other country. Family is closer to you and is more likely to know more about you (or so they think). So family knows how to hit below the belt. Family hit where it hurts. They tend to know your inner secrets and almost everything about you.

One of the earliest memories of any childhood comes from being hurt by family. Our human make-up causes us to remember more painful, hurtful events than the joyful, happy moments. A child remembers when someone has violated them in the family and being told not to say anything. A child can remember over and over again when they were picked on for being obese at family gatherings. A child can remember when everyone goes out to play, and they are left out because they can't run as fast or cannot grasp the concept of the game. A child can remember when the adults fuss because they are coming back for more food. A child never forgets when a parent says they are too big. A child never forgets a parent saying they are dumb, or that they will never be anything or never amount to anything. A child never forgets a parent saying: "You're just like your no-good daddy." A child never forgets a parent saying: "You are stupid and retarded." A child never forgets when parents fuss and yell about eating so much and call them names. A child never forgets the negative things that family always says and does to them. Why? It HURTS. It is PAINFUL and it is repeated over and over again in their mind.

From childhood through to teenage years, family constantly says and does things to create the beginning stages of what we call "hurt." This is where the crack begins. There is only so much negativity that can be poured into a person. The more that is being poured or given, the larger the crack grows. The more the molestation occurs, the crack gets bigger and bigger. It not only affects a person, but it infects that person as well. Our ego, self-confidence, and self-esteem are like sponges. We tend to absorb it all. So, if we have more negative being poured, we absorb more negativity, and our life begins to reflect that. We soak all of that in our spirit, and it affects our progress; sometimes to the point where we get stuck. If we constantly fill our bodies with foods that are not good for the body, it will begin to have a negative impact on the growth and progress of our health. For example, if we eat junk food and candy all day, every day, we will never receive the right minerals, vitamins, and other nutrients that help to support the proper functioning of our bodies. Our bodies will begin to slowly shut down and malfunction (i.e., diabetes, high blood pressure, high cholesterol). The very same thing goes for your self-esteem and confidence. If negativity is all you are hearing and being fed, then that is what your spirit will be affected and infected by. For example, if hearing that you are clumsy, fat, ugly, and no good all the time from family (those closest to you), you will eventually begin to think, act, and become just that. You will begin to question your very existence. It stunts your growth and stops your forward progress. So, the crack spreads. All this negativity affects your name and your reputation. Once planted, negativity spreads and infects you over a period of time. It causes your mental state to die and become limp, thus infecting your entire body and causing malfunction.

Family can sometimes be selfish, uncaring, and deeply inconsiderate of you. Everything they say or do only benefitting themselves. You find yourself always going out on a limb for them. You deny yourself to please them because you want to be accepted and you want to rid your life of all the negativity that has spread concerning you. In return, you get stomped on, lied on, talked about, and left out. You are the topic of every discussion at every gathering. You then begin to feel worthless and unwanted. You may even say to yourself, "Well if family doesn't want me around, who does. Nobody wants me. I am no good for anyone."

My dear friend, the enemy hears this and plays on this mentality and magnifies it in your face ten times more. The crack keeps growing. Although you are already experiencing hurt, disappointment, unbelief, mistrust within the family, the enemy uses this as a part of the game plan to keep you down and stuck. While away from family, thoughts of them still "doing you wrong" ring louder than ever in your head. The crack gets bigger.

So, you decide to stay away and not go around or get involved with family at all. Yet, you will tell them, "You know where I am if you need me." More thoughts begin to crowd your mind. You now start to see how family is treating you. Others begin to see and ask questions. You don't know how to explain, so more thoughts crowd your mind and they keep coming. The crack gets even bigger.

Then years go by without a word to family about what was said or done by them to hurt you. And yet, the hurt and pain are still there. You begin to find ways to ignore the pain you feel about it. You seek out other avenues to get away from it all. You say, "If I leave it alone, I won't worry about it or feel the pain of what happened, and it will eventually disappear." Guess what, the issue is never resolved, and the crack keeps getting bigger. Lord, how do I move on?

LIFE APPLICATION

"In prayer, there is a connection between what God does and what you do. You can't get forgiveness from God, for instance, without also forgiving others. If you refuse to do your part, you cut yourself off from God's part."
~Matthew 6:14-15(MSG)

The truth of the matter is, yes it hurts. Your heart hurts, your mind hurts, and your soul hurts. Yes, the pain seems unbearable. You cannot take it. You cannot get this out of your head. You want to throw your hands up and throw in the towel. Yes, it seems like you are the only one going through this. No one or nothing could remove the hurt, so you just do not deal with it. You just leave it alone and occupy your time doing something else; the hurt will eventually go away.

LESSON: Instead, it festers underneath the skin and becomes dangerous. Those that have hurt you may never come back to say I am sorry. They may never come back to acknowledge their wrong. Does that mean you must continue to live your life with unforgiveness, bitterness, hatred, and animosity built up?

Absolutely not!

1. Go to them. You have to dig through your pride and all those emotions of hurt and pain to go to them. You will have to speak to yourself and encourage yourself that this is the right thing to do and it is the will of God.

2. In order for you to move on, my friend, you MUST forgive those that hurt you. You forgive them, ask God to forgive you, and most importantly, forgive yourself. Too often, we beat ourselves up and say God hasn't forgiven us. Honestly, you haven't forgiven you. You MUST forgive in order to be forgiven.

3. Don't continue to hold yourself hostage. Forgive and free yourself so you can move forward in life. Seek God daily to help you in this process. Always remember kindness is the key and love unlocks the door.

WHY DOES IT HURT SO BAD?

~...and the crack continues~

Every now and then, you try to ignore the past events that keep replaying in your head. In occupying your time, you begin making time to be with friends and making new ones along the way. This time spent causes you to become closer to them. Therefore, you find yourself doing what they do, going where they go, saying what they say, and becoming just like them. All of this just to fit in. You literally hide yourself in them. Even in that, the past hurts and disappointments of family still replay in your mind. The more the past keeps playing, the more you try to hide yourself. Well, in hiding yourself, you begin to entrust those friends with your past. You begin to let your guard down and really become secure in sharing your experiences with them. They become your psychologist and consultant by telling you to just keep your mind off it, and it will go away. "Do other things so you will not have to think about it" is what they say. Their version of other things led to moments of embarrassment, such as promiscuity, drugs, alcohol, constantly wasting money, solitude, and even giving up on God. Then one thing led to another by following those friends and trying to fit in with them. Rather than fitting in, you simply stick out.

The hurt never left; it only got worse. Hurt from the past and now hurt from the ineffective pursuit of happiness as advised by those friends. The pursuit did not work. The advice given by these friends did not help rather it hurt more. The relationships did not work. Not all wrongs came out right. You gave your all, and they only took you for granted. They toyed with your emotions, played over your body, and destroyed your mind. You could no longer trust them or the friends that tried to push you to be together.

During this time, those same friends never really shared with you any of their disappointments, hurt, or pain. However, they began sharing your "secrets" with their family members who then started telling your friends and family. You just cannot lose the ones that were right there for you when you really needed them. Therefore, you began slowly trusting them once again. They not only continue telling everybody else your story, but using you like never before. They began taking your money. They were introducing you to more debt than necessary. At this point in your life, you were already so far behind financially from messed-up relationships, you did not need any more debt but keeping up with the Joneses would make it better, right?

Definitely, not.

Friends, once again, you are not able to trust. You notice they are missing when you really need them. You are wearing down slowly from more hurt from these folks that have not only betrayed you but also stole the little bit of peace and joy you did have. You could only be happy when they were happy. You could only be joyful when it was convenient for them to join in with the joy. You never really shined. You were only a sore thumb. They made sure to outshine you. You now realize those friends have been controlling you in this season. It made you more and more unhappy, disappointed, and hurt.

The pain grew. The pain became unbearable. It felt like you could not take this anymore. You threw in the towel. You threw your hands up and said this was enough hurt. You were hurting and wanted it to stop but the pain, your past, the hurt from friends; it just kept growing more and more. You wanted it to go away, but it would not leave. Many nights, you cried yourself to sleep.

You do not have anyone to talk to because now, your business is out in the streets and you do not trust anyone. You have no other option than to end it all here. Family does not love you and friends really do not care. Everyone will begin to look at you funny and call you names. Some will even walk away in fear of being isolated for their connection with you. You seem to be in this all by yourself. You think to yourself, why go through all of that and still end up alone? Why not just be alone and deal with it. No one understands and really does not care to take the time to understand. That day will be the beginning of your freedom. Freedom from people.

With a made-up mind, you need to map out how to handle it all. You have to figure out how to deal with the folks who have wronged you with a smile on your face. Each day of solitude will cause you to feel more and more alone while the hurt and pain are still there. How do you get rid of hurt and pain that hurts so bad?

When you saw, no way of dealing with it all, thoughts of ending your life and ways to do it invaded your space. You constantly said to yourself, "What will happen when you are no longer there?" As these thoughts remained and grew daily, actions soon followed. These thoughts haunted you, pictures of your past took over while you were awake, and nightmares of running from your past intruded while you were asleep. The hurt never really went away; it just silently intensified. The pain continued to grow. You ate pain, you breathed hurt, and you slept disappointment.

...and you asked, Why does it hurt so badly?

Every attempt became a failure, and you could not figure out why. Every day you walked with your head down not wanting anyone to look into your eyes and possibly know what was going on. Simply put; just trying to hide the pain. Months rolled around with you being isolated from everyone and from the world itself. You stayed to yourself and tried to be content with just that. With hopes, no one would find out the real you. You were not only hurt and in pain but now isolated, scared, and depressed. Satan used this perfect breeding ground to torture you. With this torture came more hurt and pain, thoughts of suicide and even attempts. It never became any easier. Switching faces, changing identities on a day to day basis became more and more difficult.

LIFE APPLICATION

"Casting all your care upon him; for he careth for you."
I Peter 5:7 (KJV)

The truth of the matter is that leaving "it" alone is you being a puppet to it. "It" controls you and those connected to "it" control you. This then causes you to be bound by the parameters of that hurt. The hurt eventually turns into pure pain. The pain then invites a demonic force in to hinder your maturity. It has stunted your growth.

LESSON: Leaving the issue alone does not remove the hurt. It simply causes the pain to fester becoming more dangerous to yourself and others. Deal with the issue and take the necessary steps to be healed.

1. Gather the facts. Write down only the facts of the issue/situation/matter. You may have to relive the facts by writing down only the facts. When an emotion arises, flip the paper over and write it

down as well. Remove your emotions and face only the facts.

2. Practice forgiveness daily. Each day, look at the emotional side of the paper and make a conscious effort to do and feel the complete opposite.

3. Force yourself to move on in love and humility. Take another piece of paper and for each issue/situation or act, write down a love statement that will counteract what happened.

I THOUGHT I WAS OVER IT

"Nothing matters—the crack is spreading"

Yes! Yes! Yes! It does hurt. It hurts really badly, and I want it to stop. I have tried being around others, only to add on to what was already there. I have tried leaving it alone, only to find that, too, is very dangerous. I have to release this and move on. What do I do? Aha, yes, that is it, I have the answer. I finally found the resolution. Nothing matters anymore. Just stay busy and so much so as to not let anyone or anything matter at all. Go back to school, get another job, move away, travel more, eat more, shop more, do this more, just do more.

So now, you have occupied your time with the "moreness" of life. All of your thoughts and energy are spent doing more than necessary all the time. This allows you to stay busy and not have time to think about anything. You try every sector of life doing more . . . education, shopping, eating, and traveling. You now become so busy doing more than the one thing you forgot more of was left totally out of the picture—God! Very important—the missing link. He is the most important one. Yet another Band-Aid that covered the sore of hurt and brokenness. The more you covered and did, the more the pain and hurt resonated. Everything you did ended up not working. With every chance, came a new excuse that pointed back to the brokenness. I felt it and tried burying it on the inside.

You were always told and taught the Word of God says to occupy till I come. So, you literally took that as meaning to stay busy. Now doing more becomes your intent and mission in life. The cliché becomes a reality "an idle mind is the devil's workshop." Staying busy became your daily goal. On a day-to-day basis, you denied yourself not realizing you were only destroying yourself. Doing more on the outside only made the things on the inside grow bigger. This pain has now gotten even bigger. This bandages the true feelings of hurt and pain that you still held onto.

What do you do? It still hurt? Crying yourself to sleep at night did not help. Waking up with a headache becomes a daily event. Then medicating the pain to remove the headache. Sometimes receiving some temporary relief but only for a few hours. So you continually medicate just to get some relief yet not realizing you are becoming addicted to it. It does not provide any relief or make you feel any better at all. You still feel useless, worthless, unloved, ugly, unwanted, alone, and simply not good enough.

Understanding that most of what you felt came from family and so-called friends, the next best thing is the church. Or, is it? There is absolutely safety in the church. Your time, talent, and energy now are spent in the one place where you can definitely get relief. You can definitely let your hair down . . . or can you? You disguise your issues in all that you did in the house of the Lord (Vacation Bible School, Sunday school, youth department, ushering, singing, speaking, preaching, poems, and monologues).

One day, God decides to use one of your monologues to show you exactly how you were doing the very same thing. Nothing even mattered. No one cared, no one could help, no one knew yet there were so many that were saved and delivered. As God continued to minister through you, your life now became even clearer. You are still hurting; the wound is still there and not healing. Others that truly cared were being hurt by you. There were some that really wanted to help you heal, but you cast them away. The more you did this, the more dangerous you became to yourself and to others. The wound remained open. It will not heal and is sometimes even bleeding. The crack spread!!!! Then you cry out loud, "I thought I was over it!"

LIFE APPLICATION

"But Martha was cumbered about much serving, and came to him, and said, Lord, dost thou not care that my sister hath left me to serve alone? Bid her therefore that she help me. And Jesus answered and said unto her, Martha, Martha, thou art careful and troubled about many things: But one thing is needful: and Mary hath chosen that good part, which shall not be taken away from her."

Luke 10:40-42 (KJV)

The truth of the matter is that keeping yourself busy only causes the wound to appear healed. It really forms a scab on the outside. The scab is only a cover-up. This scab can be broken. Once broken, it shows the proof of the wound never really healed and is being exposed to germs, toxins, pollutants, and infection.

LESSON: Hiding your brokenness simply hurts others. Rather than causing others to hurt, allow Jesus to heal you thoroughly. He can heal you from the inside out.

1. Stop ignoring the issue (the hurt, the pain, the disappointment). You must face the facts in order to walk in freedom. You must confront what hurts in order to conquer it. Admit it by using declarations. Face it by using different words. Yes, the name calling hurts. Yes, the bullying makes it feel worse, and it hurts. Do not ignore those things that happened to you. Yes, you were raped or molested. But you are not that victim anymore. So now you can say, "I survived being molested. I survived being raped. I survived being bullied. I survived the name calling."

2. Remove the busyness of life and of the church. Set a schedule that you will make an effort to stick to. Everything cannot be all to one end of the continuum or the next. It must be a balance. Balance is key. Being busy could also force you to be in the way. Move out of the way so God can have his way.

3. Release yourself at Jesus' feet. Lay it all at Jesus' feet. Remain humble in sharing with him all that you have held in and all you have ever felt.

4. Focus on your worship to the Father. This requires you to stay in his presence. In other words, each day you must make time for just you and the Father. During this time, focus on loving on him in a new way.

EXAMPLE: So, today, you love him for (insert your declaration) healing the loneliness. I adore the ways you have created, which causes me to know that I am loved, and I am able to love freely in return. I know that you love me, Father, because you gave your only begotten Son so that I can love others and be loved by others.

LET IT GO

~Getting past the CRACK~

After trying to do more and becoming so overwhelmed and inundated with doing stuff, the truth hits. You find out that doing stuff never really solves anything. You were only pacifying the pain and covering up the real issue. The real issue is not what happened but holding on to the hurt of what happened. The pain and discomfort of it are still there. Every day there is a reminder that pops up even though you are worn out, mentally drained, and physically tired.

Personally, I can recall a time when I was sitting on a back pew of the church during one of our Youth Explosions and all of my emotions came to the forefront. Somewhere between the start of the sermon and the end of the Bishop's message, I began to weep uncontrollably. I had held in so much for so many years, and now I was inconsolable. I was an expert at hiding my feelings. External venting was no longer a part of me because I learned how to keep it all in. I knew how to camouflage my pain, but this day, I could not. I got mad at myself for not holding it in, for letting out my secret tears, and for embarrassing myself. I no longer had a silent cry. This indescribable sobbing and weeping were very embarrassing, and everyone now knew. This was now well beyond what I came to church for. I came only to support our youth and was going to leave as soon as the preacher finished. In the midst of my sobbing, two huge arms wrapped around me and began to squeeze. I melted. I had never felt such a warm embrace before. I knew it was the Lord. How could I feel this divine embrace? It was so heavenly. The tighter the squeeze, the more I cried. I sat on that pew and cried even more. It seemed as if every tear brought a visual of the pain that I had been carrying for so many years.

Then suddenly, (yes, that Paul and Silas type suddenly) the Bishop said, "All you have to do is let it go. It is just that simple. Just let it slip out of your heart. Let it go. If you want to live, let it go." At that moment, I thought to myself, "I thought that was what I had done, that is what I am doing." Needless to say, those tears I shed came from the torture of my past (things I had done, things that were done to me, and things I had witnessed). I began to repent and ask God to forgive me. I asked him to show me a better way. I asked him to remove all those tears I shed. I asked him with a sincere heart to give me a better way.

This was a step in the right direction. I had to get past my past. I made a conscious effort every day to put the past behind me. It no longer held me hostage. Every day I could hear the Bishop's words "let it go" in my head. I made declarations each day because I knew I was done with carrying this weight. I strived every day to live out those declarations. "Let it go" became my theme and daily song. Put the old stuff behind me and live in the newness of life. After all, my past was literally killing me. There were things that caused me to hear them repeatedly in my head. Each day that I woke up, I decreed and declared no more. I decree and declared that I was done with those things and I was a new creature in Christ. I asked God every day to order my steps and teach me how to live right. After a while of doing this consistently, I no longer had those repeated visions or voices in my head. I no longer had a desire to do what gave me a thrill. I no longer had the excitement to partake of what I knew was killing me. I screamed in victory. I had seen God work in me and cause me to be an overcomer.

Those things started becoming less of an issue for me. Though I never got caught (God's grace and mercy kept me), I knew there were still things I did and was not totally honest about them. Next up, fighting internally with those things that I was not honest about. I was being dishonest to not only the victims but to myself. I started to feel that I could not even trust myself. I just knew I was on the right path until now. I thought to myself, praying and making declarations brought me out and over before, it can happen again. So, I began to pray and ask God to forgive me. Daily, I asked him to forgive me for my dishonest ways. I just wanted to be better. I just wanted to be holy. I wanted to be pure and righteous. I wanted to have the right attitude. I just wanted to do the right thing. Well, all I had to do was ask God to forgive me and he would, right?

Honesty started becoming second nature. I did not have to hide the truth anymore, and I no longer felt guilty about being dishonest in any way. Thank you, Jesus, right? Well, the day of reckoning came when my past lies caught up with me about something I stole. I began weeping sorrowfully. It was not because of the act committed but because I thought my past was over. It was done with. God had already forgiven me, and I was being honest about everything in every way. I believed literally that God threw it in the sea of forgetfulness to remember it no more. That is what we are taught, right? So, this could not be happening to me right now. Well, no one ever taught me the truths and laws of reciprocity. You know the real truth about it is that you are still held accountable for your actions. There is a big difference between forgiveness and accountability. The truth about you reaping and sowing is much deeper than money. The law of reciprocity is for the good you have done as well as the bad.

So, I had to face what I had done. I was held accountable for my fault. It was not that God did not want to forgive me, but I had to do it right; I had to confess my own fault. My portion of the wrong, my dishonesty, and everything that I had done that was not pleasing in his sight; I had to own up to it all. I then had to ask God for forgiveness from the ones I wronged. After I had taken the necessary steps in living free, I declared and even to this day, I cannot change my past. I have learned from it, and now I walk in total freedom. I am able to testify and tell of the goodness of the Lord. I am able to say that his grace and his mercy kept me. I am able to tell my story to others who may be experiencing the very same thing. The Word of God reminds us of this method of overcoming (Revelation 12:11 KJV).

One day, God instructed me to take a sheet of paper, draw a line straight down the middle, and write all that I had done. Some things were more hurtful than others. Words I had spoken over others negatively, feelings I hurt intentionally, lies I told, things I stole (time, money, and all), and even those things I omitted to do that he told me to do and say. Yep, write it all down. When I held onto tithes and offerings to go out of town. Yep, write it all down. When I accidentally walked out of Walmart with some Chapstick in the cart and did not notice that I did not pay for it, yet I kept walking. Yep, write it all down. When I came to work late, took an unauthorized extended lunch, and wrote down my "normal" time. Yep, write it all down. I was then instructed to tear the paper into shreds. God revealed to me that I would NEVER be able to piece together the shreds. With tears in my eyes, I looked at the shredded pieces as I continued to obey his instructions. I placed the shreds in an envelope in the back of my Bible. He said to me, "this is the end. It is over!" I left the envelope there and went on about my day.

Let me pause here for one moment. Sometimes, you can take every step in the right direction to make sure you have gotten over a thing and rid yourself of the very stench of it. Yet, that thing will haunt you and cause you to either second guess God's love for you or even cause you to question if God even exists. God will use the very foolish thing as your highway for help. That foolish thing that you may not even understand fully as he instructs is the doorway to your deliverance. So, never delay in obeying his instructions based on your doubts. Delayed obedience is total disobedience.

That weekend as I was assisting a friend with a wedding, God instructed me to ask for a white balloon. I got the balloon and did as he instructed. I stuffed the balloon with the shreds that were placed in the back of the Bible. My friend asked what I was doing, and I explained to her what was happening. She insisted that I give her a quick minute to do the same. She said, "We are going to do this together." She said to me, the bridegroom cannot come, and we are not ready. She went on to say, "it is during the time of decoration that we reflect on if we got our business straight. If there are any last-minute details that we omit or need to correct, we got time to get it done." We held each other's hands and walked outside together. We both watched as we slowly allowed the balloon's string to leave our hands. We also had to release the attachments of our past. What connected us to our past? We never knew where the balloon went nor did we spend the time tracing its path. We only spent the rest of the day decorating and rejoicing that God gave us another chance. It is then when you really let it go that you are no longer occupied or consumed with when it happened, where it happened, who was there, or the whys. You simply thank God for allowing you to overcome what was meant to take you out. God said, "It's finished!" With tears of joy in both of our eyes, we finally let it go.

LIFE APPLICATION

"Generous in love-God, give grace! Huge in mercy-wipe out my bad record. Scrub away my guilt, soak out my sins in your laundry. I know how bad I've been; my sins are staring me down. You're the One I've violated, and you've seen it all, seen the full extent of my evil. You have all the facts before you; whatever you decide about conceive anew, true life. Soak me in your laundry and I'll come our clean, scrub me and I'll have a snow-white life. Tune me in to foot-tapping songs, set these once-broken bones to dancing. Don't look too close for blemishes, give me a clean bill of health. God, make a fresh start in me, shape a Genesis week from the chaos of my life. Don't throw me out with the trash, or fail to breathe holiness in me. Bring me back from gray exile, put a fresh wind in my sails!
Psalm 51: 1-12 (MSG)

The truth of the matter is no matter how many times you ask God to forgive you, the law of reciprocity still exists, and you will have to face it. Facing the past first leads to you being able to let it go and live victoriously for real.

LESSON: You cannot change the past. You have to face not just what "they" did but what you did as well. Once it is faced, it is then and only then you begin to walk in total freedom. You can overcome the bondage of your past and live Free. When you are reminded of your past and tortured by the events of yesteryear:

1. Make certain you confess your part. What did you contribute to the situation? Whether it is bad words, forced actions, you must admit to what you brought to the table.

2. Ask for forgiveness

   a. From those you may have wronged (Matthew 5:23 KJV).

   b. From self – Do not beat yourself up rather grace yourself.

   c. From God.

3. Forsake the wrong – Do not wallow in it. Dust yourself off, and do not return to it. Remember with the temptation, God will provide a way of an

escape (I Corinthians 10:13 KJV). If it comes, ask God for the escape route.

4. Seek God for strength, restoration, and healing power as you walk in your freedom.

THE FLIP SIDE OF PAIN

~OH NO! It's Hard to...it is Broken~

A new day's journey and I am so glad about it. This was a new beginning for me. This new season felt rather wonderful. I never want to leave this place. As I embraced my freedom and walked confidently in my newness of life, I daily celebrated. I celebrated freedom of depression, freedom of promiscuity, freedom of dishonesty, freedom of suicidal thoughts, just simply being free. I was free to live. The Son surely made me free. What once tortured me became my praise. What once hurt me now helped me to heal.

There are two sides to every pain. It's the hurtful side and the healing side. Well, I was very familiar with the first side. No one ever really told me about or taught me about the healing. There were no seminars or retreats I could attend. No couches I could sit on free of backlash or repercussions of telling someone my business. No book I could read that gave me the truths about healing.

One thing for certain, everyone deals with healing in many different ways.

Some choose the most dangerous way, not heal at all. Those are the ones that are more likely to have nervous breakdowns or severe mental issues that lead to extended hospitalizations and sometimes death. There are those that confide in the wrong people just because they have to get it out. They tend to be the ones who seem to have a lot of dramatic experiences that cause more hurt. Those that yield to extracurricular activities such as sex, money, power, prestige, and drugs/alcohol. They do not trust anybody, so they seek other avenues. Sometimes engaged in more than one activity at a time. This too is dangerous because it can lead to prison or death. Yes, still causing more hurt. Then there are those who will internalize it all while seeking creative ways to deal rationally. They search the internet for coping mechanisms; they travel a lot by themselves, maybe they even take a ride just to breathe or a walk to get some air. These folks will go from one extreme to the other. This is where I was. I knew I never wanted to go back to the old me. I knew that was not the route I needed to take. I was running out of creative ways to heal. I started living by the old saying of "time will heal all wounds." Well, I have not mastered that one yet either because it only caused the pew (me) to break. Yes, it was hard to put on a face that I never really felt on the inside. It was no longer a crack; the pew was now broken. At this point, I was mentally exhausted, emotionally drained and abused, physically worn out, and fatigued. Overweight to severely obese, high blood pressure through the roof (top and bottom numbers in the triple digits), high cholesterol, diabetes, infertility, anemia, and a list of other ailments became my portion. So, time made it even more unbearable. I was not made whole. My emotions were healed, but by this time, my physical health was now broken and had to be healed. In an effort to walk free, I needed to not return to those things that broke my spirit, my emotions, and my very soul as I worked on being healed physically. I did not want to have a relapse, so I began to pull away from everything and everyone.

Have you ever been in a room or around a crowd and not fit in? Have you ever been around family and friends yet so far away from them? This was where I found myself so many times. So close yet so far away. My daily slogan and theme song became, I would rather be alone than unhappy. My process of healing was staying away—being distant. Distancing myself was the right thing for me to do. No one would ever know or find out this pew was broken. Yes, still in the church. I was a very important part of the church yet broken. I became many things to many people, yet I was broken. I supported the things of the church, yet I was broken. I ushered, sang on the choir, directed the choir, went to Sunday school and Vacation Bible School, yet I was broken. I preached and led worship, yet I was broken. One of the support systems of the church—a pew (me)—yet broken. It was hard for me to trust, to love, and to properly heal. Honestly, the flip side of the pain known as the healing process can sometimes hurt more than what actually caused the initial pain.

LIFE APPLICATION

He took the punishment, and that made us whole. Through his bruises, we get healed. We're all like sheep who've wandered off and gotten lost. We've all done our own thing, gone our own way. And God has piled all our sins, everything we've done wrong on him, on him.
Isaiah 53: 5-6 (MSG)

The truth of the matter is if a wound is never kept clean, it can become infected and never really heal properly or at all. There are things used to clean and protect the wound from becoming infected. Some of the things that are used to help the wound heal may burn at first but are vital to the healing process.

LESSON: Divine healing can only come through Jesus Christ alone. He is the one that was bruised for our iniquities. His blood is what cleanses us so we will not become infected or affected by our sinful and lustful desires. All we have to do is:

1. Deny self! This simply means stop having tantrums when things do not go the way we plan. Stop being obsessed with self. Move from self-centeredness to selflessness. It is okay when you are overlooked by someone you have helped. Squeezing into the spotlight does nothing but bring glory to you. Remove everything that is not pleasing to God. Rely on God for everything.

2. Accept him as Lord of our lives, our personal Savior. Ask him for help and intervention for what cannot be controlled. Do I really need to eat all the stuff that is not good for me? Do I really need to go shopping for more new clothes? Those things that we cannot seem to control, God will use as avenues to help minister to someone else, if we will seek his plan. Eating all that is not good for my body destroys the temple and decreases my movement towards destiny. I would not be of any help to others if I continue to think of it as tasting good or I have a taste for it, or it is my favorite. I could gain too much weight and cause other health issues that would hinder me from being accessible for God to use for his glory.

3. Invite Jesus to daily live in our hearts and heal our wounds—he is Jehovah Rapha, the Lord who heals. Small changes each day will cause us to live our best self in Christ Jesus. If each day we seek God's guidance and obey his instructions, we will live in a way that we are thinking more of others, and God gets all the glory and continues to heal us in the process of helping others.

4. Let the healing begin—healing of the mind (Philippians 4:8, Isaiah 26:3), body (Romans 12:1), soul (Ephesians 4:24), heart and spirit (Colossians 3:9-10). Write these declarations out. Place them in your bedroom, in your bathroom, on mirrors throughout the house, or wherever you spend the vast majority of your God time. Say them out loud every time you see them. Make these declarations of healing daily and be made whole.

BROKEN PEW

~in his presence…yet broken~

I had nowhere else to turn other than to what has now become familiar to me. The church! Yes, I went, or as some would say, I lived in the church. I was comfortable there. I found my place in the church. This was the one place my pain and my past could not haunt me. I would be hidden in the church, or so I thought. After all, Jesus threw it all in the sea of forgetfulness, right? Well, the more I went to church, the more I became the church. You ask, how is that possible? That just cannot be possible.

All the while being in church and the church could not see my pain. The church could not view what I held onto for so many years. All while I was ushering and sitting next to mothers and so many anointed people of God, and no one could see or detect or discern the suicidal thoughts running through my head. All while singing on the choir and getting my praise on, no one could see the hurt that I was hiding. No one saw that I was violated by people who said they loved me. All the while serving on so many committees, no one could see my silent cry! A cry for help. A cry to be free from mentally reliving those moments of being forced to have sex with a gun to my head. All the prayer lines I went in, very few prayed for me to be delivered from what was killing me. Yes, they prayed, but no one followed up to make sure I applied the works with my faith. No one ever taught me how to use principles and strategies along with my faith when it came to my deliverance.

So, during the times when God's glory rested in the temple, I felt his presence in the building. I saw others being delivered. I saw healing take place. I saw demons cast out. I saw other miracles performed. Yet, I was still ever so broken. I held onto secrets that were destroying my inner peace. I held onto things that I knew was not good for me. I was in his presence physically, yet broken inwardly. I began questioning the Lord. I asked him why he would not do the same for me. I asked him why was I even still here on the earth. I asked him why I could not have the abundant life he promised in his words. I began to ask when would peace ever really reside in my house—on my pew—in me.

God then reminded me that I only allowed him visitation rights. See, accepting him as my Abba Father, he had legal paternity. This is the premise for every parent who seeks parental rights to include custody and/or visitation. So who was my Father was not in question at all. In fact, he and I had a strained relationship, and our communication was off a bit. He would listen to me, but I rarely stayed long enough to listen to him. Our time together was dependent upon convenience for me. Lastly, God reminded me that my environment was not always conducive for us to spend quality time together. Many times, I had negative thoughts or things surrounding me that took away from the environment. There were too many distractions. Communication, time, and environment are all essential elements. This then established our visiting hours. I never really allowed him to reside. Yes, all those encounters in his presence, I allowed him to visit me. Each time he began getting close or near to me, I would turn the sign to close or put up the visitation hours. You may even ask how? Well, I would leave early when I felt uncomfortable. I would get up to go outside to receive a phone call or even go to the restroom. I occupied my time doing other things. I became busy in his presence which blocked him from residing. In this hour and season, we have no time for distractions. We have no time to allow God to just visit us when it is convenient for us. We must allow him to reside as he desires. It is then when he makes residence in us that Scripture assures us, he listens AND will ACT on it.

Yes, my dear friend, the more I tried to hide myself in doing ministry—being an usher, singing on the choir, youth activities, this and that, and everything else I could be consumed with—the more I occupied my time and his space. After a while of being in his presence and coming out broken, I began to pray for the abundant life that God promised us. I began to pray even harder to be like Jesus. I desired more to be the mirror image of who he was. So, I wanted to please God more and more. I constantly stayed in the face of God concerning me. I only wanted him to show me—me! I began reading his Word even more. I began to study his Word for understanding, wisdom, knowledge, and revelation even more. Not just reading, but literally with pencil and paper, searching through the scriptures and asking God to open them up to me about me. I wanted to be holy for real. I wanted to be righteous for real. I cried many nights just knowing I could have possibly done something that day that was not pleasing in his sight. As the days went on, my prayers intensified, and my song became: "Oh to be like Jesus, oh how I long to be like him."

It was then that God began to show me—me! God began to strip me of all the hurt and pain that had resided deep within me. The hurt and pain I still held was linked to some buried unforgiveness. What I realized was that the more I dug in his Word, the more his Word stayed rooted in my heart. You know, all the stuff I tried to hide, God took it away! Thank you, Jesus!!! Excuse me while I praise him once again just for stripping me. The more he stripped, the more he replaced the unnecessary layers with his Word, his peace, his joy, his gladness, and his love.

With each passing day, He gave me instructions on how to live freely.

Not only did he strip me of the pain and hurt but even the residue of it all disappeared as I grew more in him. The thought of it vanished. I could now talk about suicidal thoughts and attempts, being violated, panic attacks, anxiety, fear, no self-esteem, and so much more. My sensitivity to those things increased as I helped others battle with the things I battled with. Whenever I encountered someone who was experiencing a storm similar to the ones I did, there was no hesitation for me to jump in now and be of assistance through prayer, an encouraging word, and in any way that the Lord leads. All because it was all too familiar and now that there was no stench of hurt or pain from it all, I was stronger than ever and able to help pull my brother or sister from it as well.

LIFE APPLICATION

But if you make yourselves at home with me and my words are at home with you, you can be sure that whatever you ask will be listened to and acted upon
St. John 15:7 (MSG)

The truth of the matter is that no matter how broken you are, you must desire more of God wholeheartedly. Visitation rights are given when a noncustodial parent does not volunteer to do their part in a child's life. The courts will grant visitation so that the parent will have the opportunity to share some time with the child. Visitation is usually granted around the custodial parent's schedule. God never intended nor is he pleased with just visiting. He desires to make your heart his home. He desires to live in you. When you are of God, he will take residence in your life if you remove the "Just visiting" hours and sign from the door of your heart.

LESSON: Never allow your familiar to become your final destination. There is a huge difference in being content (being happy) and being complacent (refusing to work/seek for improvement).

1. Intensify your desire/passion for greater. Never become comfortable or complacent in your current that you refuse to do better or grow better. Get outside your comfort zone.

2. Dig deeper into God's Word. Just as you would pull out your study tools for schooling (whether you are the teacher or student), pull out your cross-reference scriptures, tablet/paper, pens, pencils, highlighters, other reference materials, etc. Jot down questions and answers. Seek Godly counsel for things you do not understand and be prayerful that God gives you a revelation about what you have studied.

3. As you grow more in his Word and allow his Word to penetrate deep within you, allow God to take residence by allowing him to strip you (no one else—just you) and completely obey

his Word and all of his commands one day at a time.

PARABLE OF PRUNING

~better, higher, more, healed…just take it away

from me~

Yes, he began breaking me to heal me. I never knew that in order to be made whole, God caused me to be broken first. This means that he will strip you of the pain of your past and every bit of trauma associated with it. You may never forget what happened or how, but you surely will not be traumatized by it as before. God still gets the glory from "it." This type of brokenness not only strips you of "it" but also of the pride of hiding it so no one will be in your business. This brokenness causes you to be humble enough to share how you got over it. This will be your testimony of what God has done, and if he did it for me, he can surely do it for you. God's brokenness allows you to see through the eyes of God and not your own. So, although it will hurt to relive what you are trying to release, the blessing of this side of brokenness is that you will now be totally healed. Simply put, you will be made whole.

This side of brokenness resembles the pruning process. Pruning is the process of weeding out any unnecessary connections/attachments that have grown from the vine. In the natural process, pruning is simply trimming, cutting back, clipping, chopping off or away. It is throwing dirt on the person's grave who violated you. It is simply getting rid of every negative word spoken over your life. Pruning is not only vital to healthy growth but to looking good as well. Although most plants have their regular maintenance, it is so important to know when to prune as well. Some may say as soon as you see some damaged leaves or a little bit of the stem dying, then go straight to pruning it.

So it is in the spirit, pruning is necessary and vitally important to our spiritual health. Much like prayer is to our everyday lives, so is pruning. We cannot be any good to the kingdom without the process of pruning.

There are some things God wants to chop off, cut away, trim up, clip, or cut back in our spiritual lives. Remember, the Word of God does remind us to die daily (I Corinthians 15:31; Colossians 3:5; Galatians 2:20;

Luke 9:23; Galatians 5:24; Philippians 1:21 KJV). If we are honest, there are times when we, too, can see areas that need pruning (even if it is after we have acted out of order or behaved not so Christ-like). For example, prematurely judging others, backstabbing, gossiping, repeating information from others that may not be all true, not showing love to everyone (turning up our nose to that drunk, that outcast, that prostitute, that crackhead and saying there is no help or hope for them). These are all actions that God has to cut away. There are times we are entertaining all the wrong people, and God has to trim the company we keep. We have connected to the wrong folk, and God has to detach us. Sometimes we can be found in the wrong places, and God has to cut those places for our good. After all, the Word encourages us to not let our good be evil spoken of (Romans 14:16-19 KJV).

Pruning never changes the fruit or the plant itself. So, God never changes whose we are or the purpose of our lives. No, it does not ever feel good, but it is for our good and makes us look better, brighter, and healthier from the inside out. When God looks at us, he wants to see himself. He does not want to see any dead or damaged things in our lives. He wants to see himself. He does not want to see that we are unable to put pride aside or that we are unable to forgive in order to uplift, edify or help our fellow man. He does not want to see that we have become so engrossed in our daily lives and in our own addiction that we have made them our gods. God wants to look in the mirror of your eyes and see himself. God in his infinite wisdom and his undying love for us, so graciously and mercifully helps us through the pruning process. His Word reminds us and tells us that he will never let us down, and he will never let us be pushed pasts our limit; he will always be there to help us come through it (I Corinthian 10:13 MSG).

LIFE APPLICATION

I am the true vine, and my Father is the husbandman. Every branch in me that beareth not fruit he taketh away: and every branch that beareth fruit, he purgeth it, that it may bring forth more fruit.

John 15:1-2

The truth of the matter is the right tool is a must when pruning. Although chainsaws work well for large trees, they are not the right tool for smaller ones. The smaller ones require a tool with a much more gentle touch. God's Word is so powerful that it can remove all the unwanted stuff without even harming us (Hebrews 4:12 KJV). Once you dive into God's Word, you will find that there are some things that God wants to get rid of in order to make us better. To go higher in him, he simply removes whatever could possibly harm us. We have to see that the pruning process is really God's Protection Plan. He wants us to be whole and have the abundant life he promised.

He wants us to be healthy both physically and spiritually, so pruning is necessary and vital to our growth in the kingdom.

LESSON: How can we be fruitful and flourish without first being broken? We have to be useful to the kingdom, so God has to remove and replace some things for his glory and for our growth.

1. Allow God's Holy Spirit to lead and guide you into all truth (John 16:13 KJV). This is how the pruning process is directed. It helps to discern our intentions and thoughts. It also encourages us and directs our minds.

2. God's timing is perfect during this process. It is difficult to realize but trust his process and plan. This could be an intervention to destroy the works of the enemy. Pray for more faith, more trust, and more belief in God's timing.

THE BLESSING OF BROKENNESS

~THROUGH IT ALL, I SURVIVED... I AM HEALED, I AM WHOLE~

Over the past few years, I have grown very fond of the HDTV and DIY channels, particularly any show about home improvement. I watched home improvements and restoration all day. I never really understood until the conclusion of this book. I never understood the 10 year plus procrastination until now. I now understand the brokenness of losing my unborn child, my son (Justun), as well as hearing God say, "It is finished" (in regard to the violation). God said the entire restoration process was to improve my creation so that he might be glorified. Though it may be your process or your story, it is for his glory. Though it is indeed painful, God still gets all the glory.

As I continued watching home improvement shows, I realized that not all houses required the same improvements. First and foremost, not all houses were the same. Some needed the electrical rewired, some required the kitchen to be redone, some required the bathroom to be gutted and completely redone (i.e., removing the tub and replacing it with a walk-in shower with a skylight window) while others only had cosmetic issues (i.e., outdated decorations, old appliances) or needed some major additions (i.e., adding a Master bedroom).

Yet, God allowed me to witness a few houses that were completely torn down. During these shows, God revealed that the land had to be cleared as well and inspected again to ensure a perfect build. Also, some of this rebuilding phase was not televised yet vital in the rebuilding process. God said some may not ever see all that you have gone through in this process to become all you need to be, but it does not mean that you are not vital or that part of the process is not important. So do not rush going through, embrace the process and know that each part of the rebuilding phase is crucial in your growth.
***

Here I am today, with a grateful heart and hands lifted in praise. God healed me and made me whole again. Every day I get up, I am determined to live better than yesterday. I wake up and walk through my house making declarations. I will not be held by my past; I decree that my best days are ahead of me. I decree and declare that my days of being a "Broken Pew" are over. I no longer hide what once hindered me. I enter into God's house and his presence with joy and thanksgiving. I am thankful to be alive. I survived all that tried to break me and destroy me. I no longer allow unforgiveness to reign in my heart. I threw dirt on that part of my past. God reminded me that I will no longer be violated, nor will I be tortured by the act or the person that did it. Rather, I rejoice because I love and can be loved unconditionally. He sent a man into my love that really loved me for me. A man that didn't want me for my body but my beauty. I know how to let things go and repent and wholeheartedly embrace others that have harmed me. I no longer hold myself captive; I live freely in victory each day. I change my atmosphere to make it conducive for a miracle. I rejoice because God restored me.

God not only restored me, but he rejuvenated, revived, and resuscitated me. God resurrected my entire life! God brought life—new life, abundant life back to me. God caused what used to be old, dried bones to live. He caused an army to rise up in me. He gave me more than I could ever ask for or dream of. God restored and resuscitated my heart. I know what real love is. I know how to love again. I know how to be loved. He revived my joy. With assurance, I can boldly say and live out his Word—the joy of the Lord is indeed my strength. He gave me his strength and peace with my past. This peace pushed me into living the abundant life he promised in my present with a greater hope for a rewarding future.

The blessing of being broken is that God can heal, deliver, set free, and restore if you follow his plan—the Word, receive his Spirit, and obey his voice. If you simply trust him and obey, God will cause you to live victoriously (Jeremiah 33:7, Deuteronomy 30:3-13). Guess what else, even when we fail God, he still restores us (Luke 22:54-62).

BROKEN TO MINISTER

I say to you today, no matter where you are in life, no matter how old you are or how long you have been broken or in "this," you can be restored. It does not matter what type of hurt, pain, brokenness you have felt or may be feeling right now, God can restore. This chapter is simply to encourage you that you can be made whole. You can live life freely. You can live off the broken pieces of what the enemy had attempted to use as your demise. If you are reading this book, your expiration date is not here. Choose today to be free and to live victoriously. It does not matter what your past looked like or who told you what yesterday. Just know that God has a better plan in store for you and he will use everything that you have ever faced, encountered or dealt with for his glory, for your growth, and for your good. Are you ready to experience a life delivered, a life free, a life full of his many blessings and all his promises? Are you ready to be content (happy) and not complacent (refusing to improve where you are)? Are you ready to smile again? Are you ready to be made whole? Are you ready to be that house built on a solid foundation? Are you that Pew in the building that needs to be fixed? God can fix that Broken Pew. He has the right bolts and screws to make certain you are sturdy, safe, comfortable, and comforting. He will equip you to handle the weight and cares of this life. He will polish you so your light can shine so brightly that men will see your good works and glorify our Father in heaven. The Blessing of Being Broken is Divine Restoration.

FREE TO BE BROKEN

Free me from the guilt and pain I feel
Free me from the heartache and hurt that won't
heal

Free me from the feeling of embarrassment and
shame
Free me from the internal struggle of blame

Free me from any responsibility I thought I played
Free me from any error in judgment I thought I
made

Free me from the mind restraints I cannot release
Free me from the firm grip of my inner peace

Free me from the feeling of haven't done enough
Free me from the feeling of inadequacy and not
measuring up

Free me from the resentment that consumes me
Free me from the bitterness that just won't let me
be

Free me from the circumstances and baggage of
the past

Free me from the loves and friendships that did
not last

Free me from the cracked pieces of my broken
soul
Free me from thinking I didn't deserve to be
mended whole

Free me from the desire to want to die in my
brokenness
Free me from thinking I had to settle for so much
less

Free me to forgive myself and others for what
they said and did
Free me to allow myself to be okay in the end

Free me to be what God called me to be
Free me, free all of me, free me from me

Lisa M. Bradley
March 2019

CONCLUSION

Precious Father, Almighty God, our Constant Healer, and Everlasting Waymaker, we pray now for every person that has sat on a Broken Pew or has been that Broken Pew. We break the cycle and thought process of Brokenness (hurt & pain) being a way of life. We thank you for the healing process. We pray that you will give us everything we need to endure the process of healing.

We pray for the victims of constant abuse (physical, mental, verbal, and spiritual). Father, we pray that you will give them the strength and strategy to seek you for a release and divine restoration.

We come against and bind up every satanic attack of brokenness in finances, families, churches/ministries and overall health of their bodies. We cancel, uproot, and denounce every foul spirit that tries to bring depression from being broken.

We decree and declare healing and wholeness in the name of Jesus. We lose the peace of God that surpasses all understanding in every situation in the name of Jesus. We speak life into what looks dead and into what has been dead for so long. We speak life to those who have lost loved ones and lost themselves in the process. We declare healing in their lives.

God, I ask that you restore each of your children reading this book. We ask for healing every hurt, every pain, every broken area, and every situation that was meant to cause harm or destruction to your children. We ask you to make each of them better in all they do so you can see yourself in them. God, bless every person that will read this and believe this prayer in Jesus name.

AMEN